2-04

HIST

D0758572

A BLUE BANNER BIOGRAPHY

Sally Field

By Russell Roberts

Mitchell Lane
PUBLISHERS

P.O. Box 196
Hockessin, Delaware 19707
Visit us on the web: www.mitchelllane.com
Comments? email us: mitchelllane@mitchelllane.com

Mitchell Lane
PUBLISHERS

Blue Banner Biographies

Eminem	**Sally Field**	Jodie Foster
Melissa Gilbert	Rudy Giuliani	Ron Howard
Michael Jackson	Nelly	Mary-Kate and Ashley Olsen
Daniel Radcliffe	Shirley Temple	Ritchie Valens
Rita Williams-Garcia		

Library of Congress Cataloging-in-Publication Data
Roberts, Russell.
      Sally Field / Russell Roberts.
          p. cm. — (A blue banner biography)
Summary: A brief biography of the actress who began her career on television as the star of "Gidget" and "The Flying Nun," and went on to become a highly acclaimed movie star, winning two Emmys and two Academy Awards.
Includes bibliographical references (p.   ) and index.
      ISBN 1-58415-183-8 (Library Bound)
      1. Field, Sally—Juvenile literature. 2. Motion picture actors and actresses—United States—Biography—Juvenile literature. [1. Field, Sally. 2. Actors and actresses. 3. Women—Biography.] I. Title. II. Series.
PN2287.F43 R63 2003
791.43'028'092--dc21
                                                    2002014334

ABOUT THE AUTHOR: Russell Roberts has written and published books on a variety of subjects, including *Ten Days to a Sharper Memory, Discover the Hidden New Jersey* and *Stolen! A History of Base Stealing*. He also wrote *Pedro Menendez de Aviles* and *Philo T. Farnsworth: The Life of Television's Forgotten Inventor* for Mitchell Lane. He lives in Bordentown, New Jersey with his family and a remarkably lazy, yet fiesty calico cat named Rusti.

PHOTO CREDITS: Cover: Globe Photos, Inc.; p. 4 AP Photo; p. 8 Globe Photos, Inc.; p. 11 Bettmann/Corbis; p. 14 Hulton/Archive; p. 19 NBC/Globe Photos, Inc.; p. 22 Bettmann/Corbis; p. 24 Shooting Star; p. 27 Rien/Corbis Sygma; p. 28 Frank Trapper/Corbis

ACKNOWLEDGMENTS: The following story has been thoroughly researched, and to the best of our knowledge, represents a true story. While every possible effort has been made to ensure accuracy, the publisher will not assume liability for damages caused by inaccuracies in the data, and makes no warranty on the accuracy of the information contained herein. This story has not been authorized nor endorsed by Sally Field.

CONTENTS

Sally Field's "You really like me!" speech at the Academy Awards in 1985. She won her second Oscar at the ceremony. Her "You really like me!" remark has been the subject of much kidding for her over the years.

A Special Night

On a spring night in 1985, a smiling, nervous, well-dressed young woman stood in front of thousands of people in a huge auditorium. Millions more were sitting at home and watching her on television.

"I can't deny the fact that you like me, right now, you really like me!" she yelled happily.

The woman was actress Sally Field. The occasion was the Academy Awards, when Hollywood honors the best actors, actresses and films from the previous year. Sally had just won the Best Actress award, or Oscar, for her role in the 1984 movie *Places In the Heart*.

Ever since that night, Sally has been kidded a great deal about her excited phrase "you really like me." Other people began saying it and making jokes about it. But the words themselves revealed how she actually felt at that moment.

Sally had been a child actress on TV, famous for comedy roles in such shows as *Gidget* and *The Flying Nun*. Now she was grown up and acting in far more realistic dramas. To her, the Oscar—which was her second—was a sign that the Hollywood people who voted for the awards really liked and respected her work as an actress. They didn't think that she should only be in simple comedy roles.

It had been a long, hard climb for Sally Field to go from light-weight television comedies to serious, award-winning dramatic movies. Along the way, she had grown from a bubbly teenager to an attractive woman in front of people's eyes on television and movie screens. But at the moment in 1985 when she stood on stage and accepted her Oscar, it's almost certain that she would not have lived her life any differently.

> *It was a long, hard climb for Sally Field to go from light-weight comedies to serious, award-winning movies.*

Acting in Her Blood

You might say that Sally had acting in her blood. Her mother, Maggie, was a former actress at the movie studio Paramount Pictures. So when Sally Margaret Field was born on November 6, 1946 in Pasadena, California, one of her parents was already very knowledgeable about Hollywood.

Her father, however, did not know much about Hollywood. His name was Richard Field and he was a pharmacist. He moved out when Sally was just four years old, and soon her parents were divorced. For a few years Sally didn't have a father. Then her mother married Jock Mahoney, a movie stuntman and actor. He eventually played Tarzan in two movies.

As a child Sally liked to watch old movies on TV and play pretend in her room with her dolls or with other children. Her mother sometimes acted, and occa-

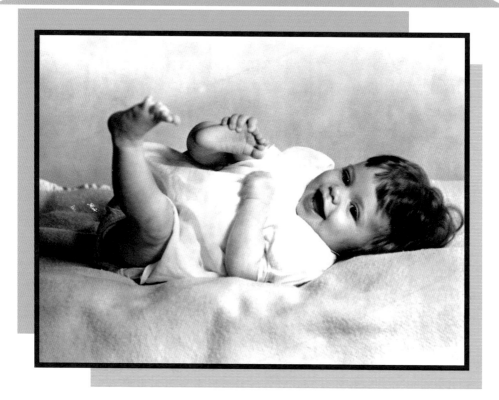

Baby picture of Sally Field. She was born in California on November 6, 1946.

sionally even took Sally to acting classes. So acting became very familiar to Sally.

When she attended junior high school, Sally was involved in numerous activities. But it was acting in the school's plays that she really enjoyed. When she was in eighth grade, Sally was selected to play several scenes from William Shakespeare's play *Romeo and Juliet* in front of an assembly of parents and guests.

She attended Birmingham High School in Los Angeles. She was a member of the Drama Club and starred in many of her school's plays. She was also voted "Funniest Girl" at her school, as well as Homecoming Princess.

After she graduated from high school, Sally planned on going to college. To keep busy over the summer, she enrolled in an acting class.

"It was just a little acting class that met one night a week," she later recalled in *Sally Field,* a book by Jason Bonderoff.

But it turned out to be very big in Sally's acting career. While standing outside the classroom one night, Sally started talking to Eddie Foy III. He was a casting director for Screen Gems, a television studio. A casting director selects people for parts in movies.

Foy asked her if she was Jock Mahoney's stepdaughter, and she said yes. He then asked her to come to his office the next day. She showed up with a big smile and wearing cutoff shorts and a tee shirt. According to Bonderoff's book, Foy thought: "She's the perfect Gidget."

And she was. Sally's acting career was born.

After she graduated from high school, Sally planned on going to college, but took an acting class over the summer.

TV Star

*G*idget was a role that Sally won after beating out 75 other actresses. It was a popular character that people knew and liked.

The character of Gidget had already appeared in three movies, played by three different actresses. Now they were going to make a TV series about her. Gidget was just like Sally in that she was a happy, beach-loving, fun-seeking, boy-crazy teenager.

The show first appeared on TV on September 15, 1965. Sally had never acted professionally before, and much was new and different to her. But the veteran actors and film crew who were making the show tried to help her as much as possible. Everyone wanted to see her succeed.

For Sally, the *Gidget* television show had two main results. The first was that it gave her some badly needed acting experience and set her career in motion.

The second was that it identified Sally with the Gidget character in many people's minds. Sally was Gidget, and Gidget was Sally. Even today, almost 40 years after the show was on TV, you can still find people who think of Gidget when they think of Sally Field.

Sally was only 18 years old when *Gidget* came on television. The show made her a "child star," the term for kids who have made it big in Hollywood. A lot of the reason the show was popular had to do with Sally herself. She was as cute as a puppy, and had a goofy, kind personality that the TV audience liked. She

Sally Field starring as Gidget. Even though the show lasted only one season, Sally has always been remembered as Gidget.

seemed more like a typical teenage girl than an actress who was playing a teenage girl. People could watch her and say, "I've got a teenage daughter just like that."

Being a celebrity also meant that Sally could date other celebrities. Among the young men that she went out with were Davy Jones of the Monkees and Gary Lewis, the son of actor/comedian Jerry Lewis.

At this point, Sally was still learning the acting profession. There was no hint that someday she'd become a great actress. But Sally wasn't the only future Oscar winner to appear on *Gidget*. In one episode, Richard Dreyfus, who later became famous in *Jaws* and many other movies, played the role of a classmate. He won an Academy Award in 1977 for his part in the film *The Goodbye Girl*.

But as good as Sally was in the role, *Gidget* lasted only one television season. It couldn't compete against *The Beverly Hillbillies*, an extremely popular show that aired at the same time on a different network.

Unknown to Sally, she didn't have to worry. There was another TV show in her future. It would last longer.

> **When Sally was cast in Gidget, there was no hint that someday she'd become a great actress.**

Fly, Girl, Fly

*T*he next show that Sally was in was called *The Flying Nun.* It was about a nun named Sister Bertrille who flew when a strong wind came along because of her hat, which looked like it had airplane wings. It also helped that she only weighed 90 pounds.

Although it was also not a big hit, *The Flying Nun* was popular enough to last three television seasons, or two years longer than *Gidget.* The show went even further than *Gidget* did in helping people recognize Sally's name and face. Ironically, at first Sally had not even wanted to make the show.

One reason was that after *Gidget* Sally had wanted to act in movies. She didn't want to do another TV show.

Another was that the first episode appeared on television on September 7, 1967. This was a time when

Sally Field in costume as Sister Bertrille in The Flying Nun. *The show gave Sally one of her most famous television roles.*

many young people were protesting against the Vietnam War and becoming very involved in politics and demonstrations. Sally, who was in her early 20s, felt foolish pretending to fly in a TV show when other people her age were involved in serious matters.

It also didn't help Sally's feelings of not "fitting in" with people her own age that *The Flying Nun* was a silly type of show. Its plots were very simple, such as the time a pelican saw her flying and fell in love with her. *The Flying Nun* was not the type of show that would get involved with some of the issues of the day, like crime, war or the environment. It was meant to be simple entertainment.

Most people did not take *The Flying Nun* seriously. They didn't take Sally seriously either, even though she tried her best. Actor Burt Reynolds once summed up how people felt about the show.

"It was a joke at the time—this person flying around with a habit [a nun's hat] on," he said, according to the website Swingin' Chicks of the 60s. "But she made it work."

Even though the two shows (*Gidget* and *The Flying Nun*) were not serious or dramatic, they did help Sally learn about acting. As she said in Jason Bonderoff's book, "Those series didn't hurt me, they gave me the greatest education in the world. There isn't anything I can't do in front of a TV camera as a result of the experience I gained from them."

The show also gave her a chance to use her singing voice, since Sister Bertrille would occasionally burst into song. Sally even made a record album that included selections from the series' soundtrack.

During this time she made a big change in her personal life. On September 16, 1968, she eloped to Las Vegas and married Steve Craig, her high school sweet-

> *Most people didn't take Sally's shows seriously. They didn't take Sally seriously either.*

heart. Early in 1969 she became pregnant. This was a big problem because the television show couldn't have a pregnant nun! So the crew had to disguise the fact that Sally was having a baby.

On November 10, 1969, her son Peter was born. After taking some time off, Sally went back to work and completed the rest of that season's shows.

After *The Flying Nun* went off the air in 1970, Sally made a few television movies. On May 15, 1972, Sally gave birth to Elijah, her second son. Shortly thereafter she starred in still another television show called *The Girl with Something Extra*. It was about a woman—Sally—who knew what other people were thinking because she had ESP (extrasensory perception).

Sally Field seemed to have everything—a nice home, money, a husband, children and television stardom.

But underneath the surface, she was very unhappy.

Although Sally seemed to have everything, underneath the surface she was very unhappy.

Sybil

*S*ally's unhappiness started with her television show. *The Girl with Something Extra* was only on for one season. Like *Gidget* and *The Flying Nun*, *The Girl with Something Extra* was a light-hearted comedy. So once again Sally felt as if she was involved in something far less serious than other people her own age.

In addition, Sally felt that acting in television comedy shows was not helping her learn to become a better actress. She desperately wanted to do important Hollywood movies, and she felt that the only way to show people that she could be a serious actress was to stop acting in television comedies.

Sally's marriage was also making her unhappy. She and her husband Steve were very different in many respects. While those differences may once have been attractive to her, that was not the case any longer.

So, after *The Girl with Something Extra* went off the air in May 1974, Sally made some changes in her life. She fired her agent and her manager, asked her husband for a divorce, and moved out of their home with her two children.

Sybil was Sally's big chance to prove that she could play dramatic parts.

For a time Sally struggled to find a more dramatic role and show what she could do as an actress. Then in 1975 she was cast in a movie called *Stay Hungry*. The part she played was a sexy receptionist who talked with a Southern accent. Although the movie wasn't a big hit, it showed people in Hollywood that Sally Field could do more than just television comedy.

Perhaps it was her role in *Stay Hungry* that got her cast in a television movie called *Sybil*. It was a true story about a woman who was mentally ill, and sometimes acted like other people — 16 other people, to be exact! The part of Sybil was far from the lighthearted comedy of *The Flying Nun*. It was the most difficult role of Sally's career. She had to express many different emotions, sometimes seconds apart, as she pretended to change from person to person.

Sally in Sybil. *The role was a radical departure from her comedy acting, and demonstrated that she was a talented, versatile actress.*

But this was her big chance to prove that she could play dramatic parts, and Sally was determined to show everyone what a good actress she had become.

The television movie was a smash hit. Sally did such a good job as Sybil that in 1977 she won an Emmy for Best Actress in a Dramatic Special. The Emmy award was significant because it was voted on by other members of the television industry.

But there was another award coming that was even more important.

Burt Reynolds and the Oscars

*I*n 1976, after she had finished making *Sybil*, Sally got a call from Burt Reynolds. He was a movie star who had made some successful movies, such as *Deliverance*. Like Sally, Reynolds had gotten his acting start in a television series—the western *Gunsmoke*. But now he was making movies, and he wanted Sally to be his leading lady in his next film, titled *Smokey and the Bandit*.

Reynolds was single, and had a reputation as a lady's man. Sally wasn't at all sure that she wanted to get involved with him or his movie. It was a light-hearted comedy about a man who drives around in a fast sports car and escapes the police. But once she talked to Reynolds, his charming ways won her over.

That started the relationship between Sally Field and Burt Reynolds. It began as friendship, but Reynolds' good looks, pleasant personality and steady supply of jokes won her over. Soon she and Reynolds were romantically involved. They were a very visible couple, always appearing together in public.

Sally and Burt made several successful movies together. The one that made the most money was the first: *Smokey and the Bandit*. It benefited from a sensational performance by Jackie Gleason as a sheriff and was the top comedy of 1977. It made more money than any other movie that year except *Star Wars*.

Sally was very happy. She was enjoying her relationship with Reynolds, and she was having great success as an actress. She wasn't exactly a threat to the great dramatic actresses of Hollywood with her comedies, but her films were making money and she was having a good time. Then she heard that a man named Martin Ritt wanted to meet with her. The results of that meeting changed her life.

Ritt was a director who had made some extremely dramatic movies in the past. Several of his films and their stars had been nominated for Academy Awards. Now he was getting ready to make a picture called *Norma Rae*, and he wanted to talk to Sally about playing the leading role.

> *Sally became romantically involved with actor Burt Reynolds. They were always appearing in public together.*

Sally in Norma Rae. *The movie, about a woman who organizes factory workers into a union so they can get better working conditions, won Sally her first Oscar.*

Norma Rae was about a poor woman living in the South and working in a factory. She becomes a labor union organizer who tries to get better working conditions for all the factory employees. The film told the story of how difficult it was for Norma Rae to organize the workers, and how she finally succeeded despite all the obstacles that were in her path.

Sally got the part, and listened carefully to Ritt's directions. The result was one of the best movies of the year. The film was a big hit and Sally was wonderful in the role. As Norma Rae, Sally sweated, struggled and strained on-screen, and really made people believe that she was a poor Southern woman working in a hot, steamy factory.

Just how good her performance was in *Norma Rae* was proven when she won an Academy Award for Best Actress in 1980. Like the Emmy Award Sally had previously won, people she worked with — this time in the movie industry — voted for the Academy Award winner. So Sally knew that those people appreciated the quality of her work.

That Oscar established Sally Field as one of the best actresses in the movies. Her long struggle to be thought of as more than just somebody who could do television comedy had finally ended. Now she was a movie star.

But as often happens, not all the news was good. Sally's Oscar and establishment as a major Hollywood star seemed to drive a wedge between her and Reynolds. The two spent as much time arguing and fighting as they did being happy together. Finally, after five years together, she and Reynolds split up in 1981.

> *Sally's Oscar and establishment as a major Hollywood star seemed to drive a wedge between her and Reynolds.*

Sally threw herself into her work to try and forget the pain of her failed relationship with Reynolds. She made several movies, such as *Absence of Malice, Back Roads* and *Kiss Me Goodbye.*

Sally with her oldest two sons. She balances both work and a personal life in the busy world of Hollywood.

But romance didn't stay out of Sally's life for long. In 1984 she got married again. This time it was to Alan Greisman, a movie producer.

The following year, 1985, Sally won an Oscar for *Places in the Heart*. She joined the short list of women who have won two Academy Awards. This list includes Katherine Hepburn and Bette Davis, two of the greatest actresses of all time.

It was at that second Academy Award presentation in 1985 that Sally gave her famous "You really like me!" speech. People remember that speech even today, and still make jokes about it.

But to Sally it was no joking matter. She had been awarded two Oscars in five years. All her life she had struggled for the respect and acceptance of the people in the movie industry. By having those same people vote her two Academy Awards, it proved to her that they did, indeed, really like her.

Sally had won two Oscars and established herself as an excellent actress who could play many different roles. What would she do next?

Sally had won two Oscars and established herself as an excellent actress who could play many different roles.

Sally Field Today

I t turned out that Sally did, and is still doing, many different things after winning her second Oscar. Just like she successfully showed people that she was more than just a television actress who could do comedy, she has showed that she can successfully do a variety of other things.

She has continued to act in movies, of course. Two of her best-known roles were as the wife of Robin Williams' character in *Mrs. Doubtfire* in 1993 and as Forrest Gump's mother in 1994's *Forrest Gump*.

She has also continued to act in television shows. She appeared as the mother of one of the characters in the medical show *ER*. In that role in 2001 she won another Emmy as the Outstanding Guest in a Drama Series. In 2002 she appeared as Justice Kate Nolan in a television show about the Supreme Court entitled *The Court*.

Sally as Forrest Gump's mother in the film Forrest Gump. *Tom Hanks played Forrest as an adult.*

It is sad but true that Hollywood tends to ignore actresses when they get older. Men continue getting good parts in movies even as they age, but older women get passed by. It seems that Hollywood only wants the youngest and prettiest girls. Plenty of good actresses have been ignored by moviemakers simply because they don't look like they're 25 anymore.

The same thing happened to Sally as she got older. So she began looking for other projects in which to utilize her skills. She directed television shows and movies. She also gave her voice to the character of Sassy the cat in *Homeward Bound* and *Homeward Bound II*. She even appeared in a television commercial that made fun of her "You really like me!" speech at the Oscars.

Sally also formed her own production company, called Fogwood Films, which allows her to make the type of movies that she wants to make.

In the meantime Sally gave birth to another son, Sam, in December of 1987. Unfortunately, her marriage to Alan Greisman did not work out, and the two were divorced in 1993.

Today Sally lives in Brentwood, California and continues to work in movies and television. Besides numerous books, her house also contains a piano and a shelf with her movie scripts bound in leather.

Sally Field has come a long way from the cute little teenager who first became a television star so many years ago. She is now an adult woman who lives quietly and works in the movie industry.

But to many people, she'll always be Gidget or the Flying Nun.

Sally arrives at the 53rd annual Primetime Emmy Awards at the Shubert Theater. She won an Emmy for her appearance in the television show ER.

CHRONOLOGY

1946	born on November 6 in Pasadena, California
1965	*Gidget* airs
1967	*The Flying Nun* first airs
1968	elopes with high school sweetheart Steve Craig
1969	gives birth to son Peter
1972	gives birth to son Elijah
1974	divorces husband Steve Craig
1976	appears in TV movie *Sybil*
1977	wins Emmy Award for *Sybil*
1979	appears in *Norma Rae*
1980	wins Academy Award for *Norma Rae*
1984	marries producer Alan Greisman; appears in *Places in the Heart*
1985	wins second Academy Award for *Places in the Heart*
1987	gives birth to son Sam
1993	appears in *Mrs. Doubtfire;* divorces Alan Greisman
1994	appears in *Forrest Gump*
2001	wins Emmy Award for her appearance in *ER*

FOR FURTHER READING

Bonderoff, Jason. *Sally Field.* New York: St. Martin's Press, 1987.

On the Web:

60s Sweethearts: Sally Field
http://www.biography.com/features/sweethearts/sfield.html

IMDb: Sally Field
http://us.imdb.com/name/nm0000398/

Swingin' Chicks of the '60s
http://www.swinginchicks.com/sally_field.htm

FILMOGRAPHY

1965	*Gidget*
1967	*The Way West*
1967-1970	*The Flying Nun*
1970	*Maybe I'll Come Home in the Spring*
1971	*Alias Smith and Jones*
1971	*Marriage: Year One*
1971	*Mongo's Back in Town*
1972	*Home for the Holidays*
1973	*Hitched*
1973	*The Girl With Something Extra*
1976	*Stay Hungry*
1976	*Bridger*
1976	*Sybil*
1977	*Smokey and the Bandit*
1977	*Heroes*
1978	*The End*
1978	*Hooper*
1979	*Beyond the Poseidon Adventure*
1979	*Norma Rae*
1980	*Smokey and the Bandit II*
1981	*Absence of Malice*

1981	All the Way Home
1981	The Making of Absence of Malice
1981	Back Roads
1982	Kiss Me Goodbye
1984	Places in the Heart
1985	Murphy's Romance
1987	Surrender
1987	James Stewart: A Wonderful Life
1987	David Copperfield
1988	Punchline
1989	Steel Magnolias
1990	Twisted Justice
1991	Not Without My Daughter
1991	Soapdish
1991	Barbara Stanwyck: Fire and Desire
1992	The Kennedy Center Honors
1992	Oscar's Greatest Moments: 1971-1991
1993	Homeward Bound: The Incredible Journey
1993	Rowan & Martin's Laugh-In: 25th Anniversary Reunion
1993	Mrs. Doubtfire
1994	Sesame Street's All-Star 25th Birthday
1994	A Century of Women
1994	Forrest Gump
1994	Through the Eyes of Forrest Gump
1994	A Century of Cinema
1995	A Woman of Independent Means
1996	Eye for an Eye
1996	Homeward Bound II: Lost in San Francisco - 1996
1997	Merry Christmas, George Bailey
1998	From the Earth to the Moon
1998	AFI's 100 Years…100 Movies
1999	A Cooler Climate
1999	Saturday Night Live Christmas
2000-2002	ER
2000	Where the Heart Is
2000	David Copperfield
2001	Say It Isn't So
2001	America: A Tribute to Heroes
2002	The Court
2003	Legally Blonde 2: Red, White & Blonde

INDEX